The Graceful Parent

Principles to Transform Your Family

with Love and Purpose

By

Katie Kattan

BOOK BOUND PRESS

https://web.facebook.com/BookboundPress/

Copyright © Peter Kattan 2024

ISBN: 979-8-3306-6006-3

First Edition: 2024

This copyright page includes the necessary copyright notice, permissions request information, acknowledgments for the cover design, interior design, and editing, as well as the details of the first edition.

Preface

Parenting is one of the most profound, rewarding, and challenging journeys a person can undertake. It is a role that demands constant evolution as we navigate the complexities of raising a child in a rapidly changing world. Yet, at its core, parenting is as much about understanding ourselves as it is about understanding our children. To become the parent our child needs, we must embark on a journey inward—exploring our own emotions, triggers, and beliefs while developing the skills to nurture, guide, and empower our child to thrive.

The Graceful Parent: Becoming the Parent Your Child Needs is not just a book about parenting strategies; it is a call to reflection, growth, and connection. Each chapter is designed to help you deepen your understanding of yourself and your child, equipping you with the tools to foster an environment where both of you can flourish. Whether you are parenting a toddler, a teenager, or someone in between, this book offers insights and practical strategies tailored to the diverse challenges and joys that parenting presents.

This journey begins by exploring your child's emotional world. Understanding and validating their emotions is the foundation of a healthy parent-child relationship. As you progress through the chapters, you'll discover the transformative power of self-reflection, the importance of building a secure attachment, and effective discipline strategies that focus on teaching rather than punishing.

As parents, we often find ourselves caught in the tension between guiding our children and giving them the freedom to grow. This book addresses that delicate balance, offering guidance on fostering independence and resilience while maintaining a nurturing presence. You'll learn to communicate with empathy, recognize the profound role of play in development, and manage the inevitable stresses of parenting.

Modern parenting also brings unique challenges, particularly in the realms of technology and screen time. This book offers practical advice on navigating these hurdles while emphasizing the importance of cultivating emotional intelligence, encouraging a growth mindset, and celebrating your child's unique qualities.

Parenting is not a one-size-fits-all endeavor. Our children come to us with their own personalities, needs, and challenges, and we, as parents, bring our own histories, biases, and dreams. By understanding the interplay between these dynamics, we can create a home environment rich in love, learning, and mutual respect.

This book is a companion for those moments when you feel uncertain or overwhelmed and a guide to inspire you to become the parent your child needs—not a perfect parent, but an intentional, reflective, and loving one. As you read these pages, may you find encouragement, practical tools, and a deeper connection with both your child and yourself.

Parenting is not a destination; it is an evolving journey. Let us take the first steps together.

With warmth and encouragement,

Katie Kattan   December 2, 2024

Introduction

Parenting today can feel like wandering through a maze, right? With all the mixed messages and pressure from society, it's easy to forget what really counts: our kids' emotional health. Every parent wants to raise happy, tough, and emotionally savvy kids, but getting there? That can be a real struggle filled with doubt and confusion. This book's here to light the way, helping you navigate the tricky terrain of modern parenting with insights that hit home.

Picture this: a space where you truly connect with your child's feelings, where you can recognize and validate what they're going through. Imagine being a parent who gets how crucial emotional intelligence is—not just for your kid but for you, too. It all starts with looking inward, figuring out your own parenting style, what triggers you, and any biases you might have. This self-reflection leads to a growth mindset, turning challenges into chances to learn.

As you dive in, you'll see just how vital secure attachments are—how being consistent and reliable builds trust and safety for your child. You'll pick up discipline techniques that focus on natural consequences and positive reinforcement instead of just punishment. Each page reveals ways to foster independence and resilience, striking that perfect balance between support and freedom so your kid can flourish.

Communication? That's the backbone of any relationship, and parenting's no different. You'll get the hang of active listening, responding with empathy, and resolving conflicts without drama. Plus, you'll discover how playtime isn't just fun—it's a key part of development, strengthening your bond and opening doors to learning.

But hey, let's be real—parenting can be tough. You'll learn how to manage stress and avoid burnout, spotting the signs that you're feeling overwhelmed. And in this tech-driven world, setting healthy boundaries around screen time and media consumption becomes super important.

As your child grows, nurturing emotional intelligence takes center stage. You'll learn to teach them emotional vocabulary, practice empathy through role-playing, and encourage them to see things from others' perspectives. A growth mindset will help both you and your child turn setbacks into stepping stones.

Transitions—big life changes or even daily adjustments—can be a lot to handle. This book's got your back with strategies to help your child cope with grief and loss, keeping things stable when life gets rocky. You'll also discover how family rituals can create lasting memories and instill important values.

Working with educators is another big piece of the puzzle. You'll learn how to team up with teachers and school staff, advocating for your child's unique needs. Celebrating diversity and embracing your child's individuality will foster respect and understanding, creating a rich family dynamic.

This journey isn't just about reaching a destination; it's about the growth that happens along the way. By following the principles in this book, you'll become the parent your child needs, armed with the tools to tackle parenting's ups and downs with confidence and ease.

So, let's dive into this enlightening journey of parenting from the inside out. Your child's emotional landscape is waiting, and together, we'll unlock the potential in both you and your kid. Welcome to a fresh take on parenting—one that honors each family's unique path and celebrates the deep connections that tie us all together.

Table of Contents

Chapter 1

Understanding Your Child's Emotional World

Kids are like little emotional sponges, soaking up everything around them. They feel, they react, and they express themselves in ways that can leave us scratching our heads. Ever had a moment where your child bursts into tears over a broken crayon? Yeah, me too. It's wild how their emotions can swing from joy to despair in the blink of an eye. Grasping this emotional landscape is the first step in becoming the parent your child truly needs. So, let's dive into three key areas: recognizing and validating emotions, the impact of emotional intelligence on development, and techniques for fostering open communication.

Recognizing and validating emotions is like being a superhero in your child's life. You might not wear a cape, but trust me, it's just as important. Kids often lack the vocabulary to express what they're feeling. They might not say, "I'm feeling anxious about school," but they sure will show it through tantrums or clinginess. So, how do you recognize those emotions?

Start by paying attention to their body language. Are they fidgeting? Avoiding eye contact? These can be signs that something's up. When you notice these cues, take a moment to acknowledge their feelings. You might say, "I see you're feeling upset about that. Do you want to talk about it?" This simple act of recognition can work wonders. It tells your child, "Hey, it's okay to feel this way. I'm here for you."

Validation is crucial. It's like giving your child a big emotional hug. You don't have to agree with their feelings, but acknowledging them goes a long way. For instance, if your kiddo is angry because they lost a game, instead of brushing it off with, "It's just a game," try saying, "I can see you're really frustrated. Losing can be tough." This lets them know their feelings are valid, and it encourages them to express themselves more openly.

Now, let's talk about emotional intelligence and its impact on development. Emotional intelligence is like the secret sauce for navigating life. It's the ability to recognize, understand, and manage our own emotions while also being aware of others' feelings. Research shows that kids with high emotional intelligence tend to have better relationships, perform better in school, and handle stress more effectively.

Think of it this way: if emotional intelligence were a video game, it would be the cheat code that unlocks extra levels of success. As parents, we can help our kids level up their emotional intelligence by modeling it ourselves. When we handle our emotions in healthy ways, we're showing our kids how to do the same.

For example, let's say you've had a rough day at work. Instead of snapping at your child when they ask for help with their homework, take a deep breath and say, "I'm feeling a bit overwhelmed right now, but I want to help you. Can we tackle this together in a few minutes?" This teaches your child that it's okay to express feelings and that it's possible to work through them without losing your cool.

So, how do we foster this emotional intelligence in our kids? It starts with open communication. If we want our children to express their feelings, we need to create an environment where they feel safe doing so. This means being approachable and ready to listen.

One effective technique is to set aside regular "talk time." It can be as simple as a few minutes before bed or during dinner. Ask open-ended questions like, "What was the best part of your day?" or "Did anything make you feel sad today?" This encourages them to share their experiences and feelings.

And here's a little tip: sometimes kids might not want to talk. That's okay! Let them know it's perfectly fine to share when they're ready. You might say, "I'm here whenever you want to chat. No pressure!" This reinforces the idea that their feelings are important and worth discussing.

Another technique is to use stories or books to explore emotions. Kids love stories, and they can be a great way to introduce complex feelings in a relatable way. For example, read a book where a character experiences a range of emotions and then discuss it together. Ask your child how they think the character felt and what they might have done differently. This not only helps them understand emotions but also builds empathy.

Now, let's get a bit practical. Here are some actionable steps you can take to dive deeper into your child's emotional world:

1. Practice Active Listening: When your child talks, give them your full attention. Put down your phone, make eye contact, and nod to show you're engaged. It's like giving them a spotlight to shine in.

2. Use Emotion Labels: Help your child build their emotional vocabulary. Instead of just

saying, "Are you sad?" try using a range of feelings like "frustrated," "excited," or "worried." This helps them articulate their emotions better.

3. Model Emotional Regulation: Show your child how to handle emotions constructively. If you're feeling angry, express it calmly. "I'm feeling really upset right now, but I'm going to take a few deep breaths to calm down."

4. Create a Feelings Chart: Make a fun chart with different emotions and faces. When your child is feeling something, they can point to the chart. It's a great visual aid to help them communicate.

5. Encourage Journaling: If your child is old enough, encourage them to keep a feelings journal. Writing down their thoughts can be a powerful way to process emotions. Plus, it's a

great way to get to know what's going on in their minds.

6. Practice Empathy: Teach your child to consider others' feelings. When they see someone upset, ask them how they think that person feels and what they could do to help. It's like training for emotional superheroes!

Now, I know what you might be thinking: "But what if my kid just won't talk?" Trust me, I've been there. Sometimes it feels like pulling teeth to get them to open up. Here's the deal: keep trying. The more you create a safe space for communication, the more likely they'll eventually come around.

And don't forget about the power of play. Kids often express their feelings through play. Watch how they interact with their toys or engage in role-playing games. You might discover a lot about their emotional world just by observing.

In conclusion, understanding your child's emotional world isn't just about recognizing their feelings; it's about creating a foundation for emotional intelligence that will serve them for life. By validating their emotions, modeling healthy emotional responses, and fostering open communication, you're setting your child up for success.

So, the next time your child has a meltdown over something that seems trivial to you, take a breath and remember: their feelings are REAL. Embrace the chaos, laugh at the absurdity, and keep those lines of communication wide open. You've got this, and your child will thank you for it in ways you can't even imagine yet. Let's get out there and be the parents our kids need!

Chapter 2

The Power of Self-Reflection

Self-reflection in parenting? Sounds fancy, huh? But trust me, it's the secret sauce to being the parent your kid really needs. It's all about looking in the mirror and asking, "What's my deal?" Let's break it down into three key areas: figuring out your parenting style, recognizing your triggers and biases, and fostering a growth mindset. Buckle up; it's gonna be a ride!

First up, let's talk about your parenting style. Ever stop to think about how you actually parent? Maybe you're a strict enforcer or a laid-back adventurer. Or maybe you're a mix, picking and choosing like it's a parenting buffet.

Here's the deal: knowing your style can help you tackle parenting with more confidence.

So, how do you figure it out? Start by asking yourself some questions. What do you value most in raising your kid? Independence? Structure? Emotional connection? Write it down—think of it as your parenting manifesto! You might be surprised by what you find out.

Now, let's dig a little deeper. Consider how your own upbringing shapes your style. Did your parents run a tight ship, or was it more "let's see what happens"? Our past experiences really influence how we parent. If your folks were strict, you might rebel by being more lenient. Or the opposite! It's a cycle, and breaking it starts with awareness.

Once you get a grip on your style, it's time to tackle your triggers and biases. Oh boy, this one's a doozy. We all have those moments when our kids push our buttons, right? Maybe it's when they ignore you or throw a fit in the store. Instead of blowing up like a volcano, step back and ask yourself, "Why am I feeling this way?"

That's where self-reflection comes in. Recognizing your triggers helps you respond thoughtfully instead of reacting on impulse. For example, if you get cranky when your kid makes a mess, it might be linked to your need for order. That's cool; it just means you gotta find a balance. Maybe set a cleanup time or involve your kid in the process. Make it a game! Who doesn't love a little competition?

Now, let's chat about biases. We all have 'em, whether we wanna admit it or not. Maybe you have a bias against certain behaviors because of your own childhood. If you got punished for being loud, you might find yourself shushing your kids when they get excited. Take a moment to think about those biases. Are they helping or hurting your parenting? Remember, your kid deserves a safe space to express themselves—even if it gets a bit noisy.

Alright, let's shift gears and talk about developing a growth mindset for parenting. You've probably heard that term tossed around, but what does it mean? Simply put, it's the belief that you can grow and improve through effort and learning. This mindset is crucial for both you and your child. Think of it like planting a seed and watching it blossom!

To grow that mindset, start by embracing challenges. Parenting's full of 'em—trust me! Instead of seeing setbacks as failures, view them as chances to learn. Maybe you had a rough day and lost your cool. Instead of beating yourself up, think about what you could do differently next time. Maybe take a deep breath or step outside for a quick reset. It's all about progress, not perfection.

And don't shy away from feedback. This can come from your partner, friends, or even your kids. Yep, I said it! Ask your kids how they feel about your parenting. They might surprise you with their insights. "Mom, I love it when you play with me instead of just telling me what to do." Boom! That's golden feedback. It shows you where you can improve and grow.

Now, let's get practical. Here's a quick action plan to harness self-reflection in your parenting journey:

1. Identify Your Parenting Style

   - Reflect on your values and upbringing.

- Jot down your thoughts and create a parenting manifesto.

2. Understand Your Triggers and Biases

- Recognize what sets you off and why.

- Reflect on your biases and how they impact your parenting.

3. Develop a Growth Mindset

- Embrace challenges and view setbacks as learning opportunities.

- Seek feedback from your kids and those around you.

Remember, self-reflection isn't a one-and-done deal; it's a lifelong process. Make it a habit to check in with yourself regularly. Maybe set aside a few minutes each week to journal your thoughts or have a heart-to-heart with your partner. This practice will keep you grounded and focused on being the parent your child truly needs.

And hey, if you feel overwhelmed, that's totally normal! Parenting's like juggling flaming torches while riding a unicycle—no easy feat! Cut yourself some slack and remember that growth takes time. Celebrate the small wins. Maybe you handled a tough situation better than you would've last week. That's progress!

In the end, self-reflection is all about understanding yourself so you can be the best parent possible. It's not just about your kid's emotional world; it's about yours too. You're on this journey together, learning and growing side by side. So, take a deep breath, grab a cup of coffee (or tea, if that's more your style), and dive into the beautiful chaos that is parenting. You got this!

Chapter 3

Building a Secure Attachment

Alright, let's get into the nitty-gritty of parenting. Building a secure attachment with your kid is like setting the groundwork for a skyscraper. You wouldn't skimp on the concrete, right? Same deal with your bond. Consistency and reliability? Absolutely crucial. Kids need to know you're their safety net, ready to catch them when they fall—like a circus act.

Picture this: your kid spills juice or has a meltdown over a broken toy. How you handle it shapes their world. If you're always there, comforting them, they'll learn to trust you. It's like constructing a bridge—every supportive moment adds another plank. Eventually, that bridge becomes strong enough for them to venture into independence and resilience.

Now, let's chat about how to nurture that trust and safety. First up, be present. And I don't mean just being in the same room while scrolling through your phone. I mean really engaging. Put that device down, make eye contact, and listen. Ask about their day, dive into their stories, and show you care. When they see you're genuinely interested, you're building a bond that's tough to break.

Next, establish routines. Kids dig routines like I dig a good slice of pizza. It gives them a sense of control and predictability. Whether it's a bedtime story or Sunday pancake breakfast, keep it consistent. These little rituals wrap them in a sense of safety, like a warm blanket on a cold night.

But hey, I know what you're thinking: "What if I screw up?" You will. We all do. The trick? Own it. If you lose your cool, apologize. Show your kid it's okay to mess up and that owning your mistakes is a strength, not a weakness. It's like giving them a front-row seat to the beautiful mess of life.

Now, let's dig into how attachment styles shape future relationships. Buckle up; this part's juicy. Research shows that how we attach to our caregivers as kids influences our adult relationships. If you nail that secure attachment, your kid's more likely to form healthy bonds later on. They'll know how to trust, communicate, and connect. It's like handing them a toolkit for life.

On the flip side, if a kid grows up with inconsistent responses, they might end up with an anxious or avoidant attachment style. Imagine trying to build a sandcastle, but every time you get close, the tide washes it away. Frustrating, right? These kids may struggle with trust and intimacy in their future relationships.

So, how can you help your kid steer clear of that? Keep that bridge strong! Encourage open communication and validate their feelings. If they're upset, don't brush it off. Instead, say, "I see you're feeling sad. Want to talk about it?" This not only nurtures their emotional intelligence but also reinforces that their feelings matter.

Here's a quick checklist to help you build that secure attachment:

- Be Consistent: Show up for your kid. Whether it's a soccer game or a simple dinner chat, be there.

- Establish Routines: Create rituals they can look forward to.

- Communicate Openly: Ask questions and listen. Make them feel heard.

- Acknowledge Mistakes: If you slip up, own it. Show them it's okay to be imperfect.

- Encourage Independence: Give them space to explore, knowing you're there to catch them if they fall.

And don't forget the magic of play. Kids learn a ton about relationships through playtime. So, jump in! Play pretend, build a fort, or have a silly dance-off in the living room. These moments strengthen your connection and trust, showing them you're a safe space to express themselves.

In the end, building a secure attachment isn't just about the big moments. It's in the everyday interactions, those little gestures of love and understanding. It's about creating a home where your kid feels safe to explore the world and, in turn, build healthy relationships outside of it.

So, take a deep breath and remember: you've got this! Every moment you invest in your kid is like watering a plant. With time, love, and care, they'll blossom into the incredible person they're meant to be. Now, go out there and build that bridge—one plank at a time!

Chapter 4

Effective Discipline Strategies

Discipline. Just saying it might make you cringe, huh? You probably picture some strict teacher with a ruler, but hold up! Discipline and punishment? Totally different beasts. They're like comparing apples to oranges. One's sweet and comforting, the other? Not so much.

So, what's the scoop on discipline? It's all about teaching your kid to make better choices—not just slapping them with a consequence when they mess up. Think of it as steering a ship. You want to guide them, not toss 'em overboard when they hit a rough patch. You're the captain, navigating the choppy waters of childhood with style and purpose.

Let's break it down. Discipline has two main parts: natural and logical consequences. Natural consequences happen because of a child's actions. If your kid refuses to wear a jacket on a chilly day, they'll feel the cold. It's a straightforward lesson that sticks. Logical consequences are a bit more organized. If your kid scribbles on the walls, a logical consequence would be having them help clean it up. This isn't about punishing them; it's about teaching responsibility. They need to see that their actions have real effects.

Now, you might be wondering, "What if they just don't get it?" That's where positive reinforcement steps in. It's like the cherry on top of your parenting sundae. When your kid does something good, shout it out! Praise them, give a high-five, or even bust a little dance. Seriously, it works like magic. Positive reinforcement encourages your child to keep up the good behavior. It's not just about dodging the bad stuff; it's about celebrating the good, too.

Let's hit some stats. Research shows that kids who get consistent positive reinforcement are way more likely to show desired behaviors. One study even found that positive reinforcement can boost the chance of a behavior being repeated by up to 80%. That's a big deal! So, if you're not on this train yet, what's holding you back?

Here's a quick story. My buddy Dave has a son, Timmy, who was a handful. Timmy loved testing limits—like a little daredevil. Instead of jumping to consequences, Dave decided to switch it up. He started praising Timmy for good choices, like helping his sister or cleaning up his toys without being asked. The change was wild! Timmy thrived on that praise. It was like he was collecting gold stars, and who doesn't love a good gold star?

So, let's recap. Discipline is about teaching and guiding. Natural and logical consequences are your tools for helping your child learn from their actions. And positive reinforcement? That's the secret sauce that makes it all stick.

Now, here's a challenge for ya: This week, try to use at least one of these strategies. Maybe focus on giving more praise, or start using logical consequences instead of jumping straight to punishment. Whatever it is, be intentional. Remember, you're not just raising kids; you're shaping future adults. That's a big responsibility!

Feeling overwhelmed? Don't sweat it. You're not alone. Parenting's a wild ride, and it's okay to throw your hands up and scream sometimes. Just remember, you're in control of this rollercoaster. So buckle up, take a deep breath, and let's tackle this journey together. You got this!

Chapter 5

Encouraging Independence and Resilience

Ah, parenting! It's a wild ride, isn't it? One minute you're the hero in your child's eyes, and the next, you're just the one who won't let them have dessert before dinner. But here's the kicker: our ultimate goal as parents isn't just to be their best buddy or the dessert police. Nope, we're here to help them grow into independent, resilient little humans. So, let's dive into how we can strike that delicate balance between support and autonomy, teach problem-solving skills, and foster a growth mindset through challenges. Buckle up, folks—this is gonna be good!

First off, let's chat about the balance between support and autonomy. Imagine you're at a carnival. You've got your kiddo holding onto the edge of the merry-go-round, eyes wide with excitement and a hint of fear. Do you rush in and grab them? Or do you let them take a spin on their own? It's a tough call! The trick is to offer just the right amount of support without being overbearing. Think of it as being their safety net, not their parachute.

When your child is trying something new—like riding a bike or making a new friend—be there to cheer them on. But let them take the lead. Encourage them to try it out, and when they wobble or fall, remind them that it's all part of the process. Here's a little tip: ask open-ended questions like, "What do you think you could do differently next time?" This not only encourages them to think for themselves but also shows that you believe in their ability to figure things out.

Now, let's talk about teaching problem-solving skills. This is where the rubber meets the road, folks! Life is a series of challenges, and we want our kids to tackle them head-on. You know that saying, "Give a man a fish, and you feed him for a day; teach a man to fish, and you feed him for a lifetime"? Well, it applies here too! Instead of swooping in to fix every little issue, let's guide our kids through the problem-solving process.

Next time your child faces a dilemma—maybe they can't find their favorite toy or they're struggling with a math problem—encourage them to brainstorm solutions. Ask them, "What are some ways you could solve this?" You'll be amazed at the creativity they'll unleash! Maybe they'll come up with a plan to search the house or even create a math rhyme to remember the steps.

And here's a fun idea: turn problem-solving into a game! Set up scenarios where they have to think on their feet. You could create a "Problem-Solving Olympics" at home, where they earn points for each solution they come up with. Trust me, this will not only build their confidence but also make them feel like they're conquering the world—one challenge at a time!

Now, let's not forget about fostering a growth mindset through challenges. This is where we get to sprinkle some magic dust on our parenting. You see, a growth mindset is the belief that abilities can be developed through dedication and hard work. It's like turning your kid into a little superhero, ready to tackle any challenge that comes their way!

So, how do we do this? First, model a growth mindset yourself. Share your own challenges and how you overcame them. Remember that time you tried to bake a soufflé, and it turned into a pancake? Laugh about it! Show your kids that failure isn't the end of the world; it's just a stepping stone to success.

Encourage them to embrace challenges instead of shying away from them. When they say, "I can't do this," flip the script! Respond with, "You can't do it YET!" This simple shift in language can make a world of difference. It plants the seed that effort leads to improvement.

Celebrate their efforts, not just the results. Did they work hard on a school project, even if the grade wasn't what they hoped for? Praise them for their dedication! Let them know that the process is just as important as the outcome. You might even want to create a "Growth

Mindset Wall" at home, where you can post achievements, big or small.

And here's a little nugget of wisdom: challenges are like the gym for the brain. The more you push it, the stronger it gets. So, when your child faces a tough situation, remind them that they're building their resilience muscles.

To wrap it all up, encouraging independence and resilience in our kids is all about finding that sweet spot between support and autonomy. It's about teaching them to tackle problems head-on and embracing challenges as opportunities for growth.

Here's a quick recap to keep you on track:

1. **Balance Support and Autonomy**

    - Be their safety net, not their parachute.

- Ask open-ended questions to encourage independent thinking.

2. **Teach Problem-Solving Skills**

- Guide them through dilemmas instead of fixing them.

- Turn problem-solving into a fun game or challenge.

3. **Foster a Growth Mindset**

- Model a growth mindset through your own experiences.

- Celebrate efforts and create a "Growth Mindset Wall."

Remember, you're not just raising kids; you're raising future adults who can navigate life's ups and downs. So, go out there and be the supportive guide they need while giving them the freedom to soar. You've got this! And hey, if you ever feel overwhelmed, just remember: even the best parents have days when they're winging it. Keep it real, keep it fun, and most importantly, keep it loving.

Chapter 6

Communicating with Empathy

Let's dive into a topic that's as crucial as knowing when to say "no" to your kid's sixth cookie of the day—COMMUNICATION. But not just any kind of communication. We're talking about the art of communicating with empathy. It's like being a ninja in the parenting world. You need to be stealthy, observant, and ready to respond with precision. So grab a cup of coffee, or maybe a glass of wine (I won't judge), and let's get into it.

First up is the art of active listening. Now, I know what you're thinking: "What's so special about listening?" Well, let me tell you, my friend, active listening is like the secret sauce in your parenting recipe. It's not just about hearing the words your child is saying; it's about tuning into their feelings, emotions, and the little nuances that often get lost in translation.

Picture this: your kid comes home from school, and they're all worked up because they didn't get picked for the team. Instead of jumping straight into problem-solving mode, try this little trick: put down your phone, look them in the eye, and give them your full attention. Nod your head, use affirming sounds like "uh-huh" or "I see," and resist the urge to interrupt. It's like being a therapist but without the fancy degree.

Here's a quick list of active listening techniques to try:

1. **Make Eye Contact**: This shows your child that you're genuinely interested.

2. **Use Open Body Language**: Lean slightly forward, and avoid crossing your arms. You want to be approachable, not like a bouncer at a club.

3. **Reflect Back**: Paraphrase what they say. "So, you're feeling sad because you didn't make the team?" This not only validates their feelings but also helps you understand their perspective better.

4. **Ask Open-Ended Questions**: Instead of "Did you have a good day?" try "What was the best part of your day?" This encourages them to share more.

Now, let's move on to responding to your child's needs with empathy. It's one thing to listen, but it's another to respond in a way that truly meets their emotional needs. Think of empathy as your parenting superpower. When you respond with empathy, you're not just addressing the surface issue; you're diving deep into the emotional waters where your child's feelings reside.

For instance, if your child is upset about a friend who didn't invite them to a birthday party, instead of brushing it off with "Oh, it's no big deal," try saying something like, "I can see why you'd feel hurt. It's tough when friends don't include us." This simple acknowledgment can make a world of difference. It's like throwing a life raft to someone who's floundering in the ocean of their emotions.

Here are some tips for responding empathetically:

- **Validate Their Feelings**: Let them know it's okay to feel what they're feeling.

- **Avoid Dismissing Their Emotions**: Even if it seems trivial to you, it's monumental to them.

- **Share Similar Experiences**: If you've been in a similar situation, share it! It helps them feel less alone. Just don't turn it into a "let me tell you about my day" moment. Keep the focus on them.

Now, let's tackle the elephant in the room: conflict resolution. Because let's face it, conflicts are as inevitable as a rainy day in April. But here's the kicker—conflicts don't have to end in World War III. With the right techniques, you can resolve conflicts peacefully and maybe even come out stronger as a family.

One effective method is to use "I" statements instead of "you" statements. For example, instead of saying, "You never listen to me!" try, "I feel ignored when I'm talking and you're on your phone." This shifts the focus from blame to expressing your feelings, which can help defuse tension.

Here's a simple framework for resolving conflicts:

1. **Identify the Problem**: Both parties need to agree on what the issue is.

2. **Express Feelings**: Each person shares how they feel about the situation without interruption.

3. **Brainstorm Solutions Together**: Get creative! Maybe there's a compromise that works for everyone.

4. **Agree on a Solution**: Make sure everyone is on board. Write it down if you need to.

5. **Follow Up**: Check in later to see how things are going. It shows you care and are invested in the solution.

Remember, conflict resolution isn't just about finding a solution; it's about teaching your child valuable skills for handling disagreements in the future. You're not just parenting; you're equipping them for life.

So, as we wrap this up, let's recap the essentials of communicating with empathy:

- Active listening is your first step. Tune in, engage, and reflect.

- Responding with empathy shows your child that their feelings matter. It builds trust and connection.

- Conflict resolution techniques can turn potential disasters into opportunities for growth.

Now, here's a little challenge for you: This week, pick one of these techniques and put it into practice. Maybe it's listening more intently, responding with empathy, or resolving a conflict using "I" statements. Whatever it is, commit to it. You might just find that these small changes can lead to BIG improvements in your relationship with your child.

So go on, channel your inner parenting ninja, and communicate with empathy. Your child will thank you for it, and you might just find that you're learning a thing or two about yourself along the way. Happy parenting!

Chapter 7

The Role of Play in Development

Playtime, huh? It's not just for the kiddos! If you think play's just a way for kids to kill time, you're seriously missing out. Unstructured play is like the Swiss Army knife of childhood—super versatile, essential, and a whole lotta fun! Let's break down why play is a must for your little ones and how it can strengthen your bond.

First, let's chat about unstructured play. You know, that magical moment when your kid can explore, imagine, and create without a schedule? It's like letting a wildflower grow in a garden of strict hedges. Unstructured play sparks creativity, boosts problem-solving skills, and lets your child learn at their own pace. Plus, it's a breather for you! You can chill with a coffee (or maybe a sneaky glass of wine) while your kid builds a fort from couch cushions. Win-win, right?

Now, you might be asking, "How much unstructured play is enough?" Well, the American Academy of Pediatrics says kids need at least 60 minutes of active play daily. But don't stress about scheduling it! Just let them run wild in the backyard or get messy with art supplies. Trust me, the mess is totally worth it. Studies show kids who play freely develop better social skills and emotional intelligence. So, you're not just letting them have fun; you're helping them grow into well-rounded humans.

Next up, let's talk about mixing in some educational play. I know, I know—"Educational play? Sounds boring." But hold on! It doesn't have to feel like homework. You can turn bath time into a science experiment or use board games to sneak in some math skills. Kids learn best when they're having a blast, so get creative!

Here's a quick rundown of ways to add some educational play to your day:

1. **Storytime Adventures**: Read together, but don't just read—act it out! Use props, change voices, make it interactive. Your kid will be engaged, and they might pick up a thing or two about storytelling.

2. **Cooking Together**: Get your little chef in the kitchen. Cooking teaches measurements, following directions, and even some science (hello, chemical reactions!). Plus, you get to eat the results—score!

3. **Nature Walks**: Take a stroll and turn it into a scavenger hunt. Make a list of things to find—like a red leaf or a smooth rock. This gets them moving and teaches them about the world.

4. **Art Projects**: Let your kid create art with all sorts of materials. It's a great way for them to express themselves and develop fine motor skills. Plus, you can sneak in lessons about colors and shapes!

5. **Role-Playing Games**: Whether they're superheroes or running a restaurant, role-playing helps kids see different perspectives and build empathy. Plus, it's a blast to join in!

The trick? Keep it light and playful. If you're having fun, they will too. That's what matters!

Now, let's shift gears and see how play can strengthen your bond with your child. Play is like glue for your relationship. It builds trust, boosts communication, and creates lasting memories. When you play with your kid, you're showing them you care about their interests and want to invest time in their happiness. That's a big deal!

Think back to your own childhood. What do you remember? Was it studying for tests or playing games with family? Bet it's the latter! Those shared moments create a sense of belonging. When you play together, you're not just having fun; you're laying the groundwork for a solid parent-child relationship.

Here are some tips to maximize your playtime:

1. **Be Present**: Ditch the phone and distractions. Give your kid your full attention. They'll feel valued, and you'll enjoy the moment more.

2. **Follow Their Lead**: Let your child steer the play. If they wanna build a spaceship outta Legos, go for it! This shows their ideas matter and sparks creativity.

3. **Share Laughter**: Humor's a great bonding tool. Make silly faces, tell jokes, engage in playful banter. Laughter creates a positive vibe and helps your kid feel safe and loved.

4. **Try New Things**: Step outta your comfort zone! If your kid wants to try something new, be open. Whether it's a new game or sport, your willingness to join in shows you're all in.

5. **Reflect Together**: After playtime, chat about what you did. Ask your kid what they enjoyed most or learned. This reinforces the experience and encourages communication.

By embracing play in your parenting journey, you're giving your child the gift of exploration, creativity, and connection. It's like handing them a toolbox filled with skills for life. And who knows? You might learn a thing or two along the way!

So, let's wrap this up. Here's a quick recap on why play is key for your child's development:

- Unstructured play boosts creativity, problem-solving, and social skills.

- Educational play can be fun and easily mixed into daily routines.

- Play strengthens the parent-child bond, building trust and lasting memories.

So go ahead—let your kid play! Encourage them to explore, imagine, and create. And don't forget to jump in on the fun yourself. You'll be amazed at the magic that happens when you embrace play in your parenting journey. Now, who's up for a game of tag?

Chapter 8

Managing Stress and Burnout

You know, parenting is a wild ride. One minute, you're basking in the glow of your child's sweet smile, and the next, you're wondering if you've just accidentally signed up for a marathon of chaos. Sound familiar? Let's get real about something that's often swept under the rug: parental burnout. It's a thing, and it can hit you like a ton of bricks if you're not careful.

Recognizing signs of parental burnout is crucial. Picture this: you wake up, and the idea of facing another day of tantrums, homework, and the endless cycle of laundry makes you want to crawl back under the covers. You're not alone! Many parents feel this way, but it's essential to recognize these feelings before they spiral out of control.

So, what are some signs you might be experiencing burnout? Here's a handy checklist:

1. **Constant Fatigue**: You feel like you've run a marathon, but you haven't even left the house.

2. **Irritability**: Little things that used to roll off your back now send you into a tailspin. Did your kid just ask for a snack? Cue the eye roll.

3. **Lack of Motivation**: You can't muster the energy to play that board game for the fifth time this week.

4. **Feeling Overwhelmed**: The thought of planning a simple family dinner feels like climbing Mount Everest.

5. **Emotional Detachment**: You find yourself zoning out during family activities. It's like you're there, but not really there.

If you're nodding along to this list, it's time to hit the brakes and take a step back. Recognizing these signs is the first step in combating burnout.

Now, let's talk about strategies for self-care and stress management. It's like putting on your oxygen mask before helping your child with theirs. You can't pour from an empty cup, folks! Here are some practical tips to help you recharge your batteries:

- **Set Boundaries**: It's okay to say no. Whether it's to a playdate or an extra chore, protect your time. You're not a superhero, and even superheroes need a break.

- **Schedule 'Me Time'**: Carve out some time for yourself—yes, you! Whether it's a long bath, a quick jog, or binge-watching that show everyone's talking about, prioritize it. Set a timer if you have to. You deserve it!

- **Practice Mindfulness**: Take a moment to breathe. Seriously, just breathe. Mindfulness can help ground you and reduce stress. Try meditating for five minutes a day. You might be surprised at how much clarity it brings.

- **Stay Active**: Physical activity is a game-changer. It doesn't have to be an intense workout—just a walk around the block can do wonders for your mood. Think of it as a mini-vacation from parenting.

- **Get Enough Sleep**: I know, I know. Easier said than done, right? But try to prioritize sleep. It's the foundation of your well-being. If you can, sneak in a nap when the kids are napping. You'll thank yourself later.

- **Seek Professional Help**: If you're feeling really overwhelmed, don't hesitate to reach out to a therapist or counselor. There's no shame in asking for help. It's a sign of strength, not weakness.

Now, let's shift gears and talk about building a support network for parenting challenges. You don't have to go through this alone! Surrounding yourself with a solid support system can be a game-changer. Here's how to build that network:

- **Connect with Other Parents**: Find your tribe! Join a local parenting group or connect with other parents online. Sharing experiences can lighten the load and remind you that you're not alone in this crazy journey.

- **Lean on Family and Friends**: Don't be afraid to ask for help from family and friends. Whether it's babysitting, a listening ear, or even a home-cooked meal, let them support you. They want to help; they just might not know how.

- **Create a Parenting Co-op**: Team up with other parents to share responsibilities. You take the kids on Tuesday, and they take them on Thursday. It's a win-win situation!

- **Utilize Community Resources**: Many communities offer parenting classes, workshops, or support groups. Take advantage of these resources. They can provide valuable insights and a sense of camaraderie.

- **Be Open About Your Struggles**: Vulnerability can be powerful. Share your parenting challenges with others. You'll likely find that many parents are facing similar issues, and it can foster deeper connections.

In wrapping up this section, let's take a moment to reflect. Parenting is a journey filled with ups and downs. Recognizing the signs of burnout, implementing self-care strategies, and building a support network are all essential steps in managing the stress that comes with it.

So, what's your next move? Take a deep breath and make a plan. Choose one self-care strategy to implement this week. Maybe it's scheduling that 'me time' or reaching out to a friend for support. Whatever it is, take action. You've got this!

Remember, you're not just a parent; you're a human being with needs, dreams, and a right to happiness. Embrace the chaos, lean on your support network, and don't forget to laugh along the way. After all, parenting is a wild ride, and it's okay to enjoy the journey—burnout and all!

Chapter 9

Navigating Screen Time and Technology

Let's dive into the digital jungle that is parenting in the age of screens. If you're like me, you've probably found yourself scrolling through your phone while your kiddo is glued to their tablet, and you're left wondering, "Is this normal?" Spoiler alert: it is! But just because it's common doesn't mean it's ideal. So, grab a snack and let's unpack how to set healthy boundaries, understand the impact of technology on development, and encourage balanced media consumption.

First things first, let's talk about setting healthy boundaries for device usage. This is like putting up a fence around a beautiful garden. You want to keep the weeds out while still allowing the flowers to bloom. Kids today are surrounded by screens—tablets, smartphones, TVs, you name it. And while technology can be a great tool for learning and creativity, too much of it can lead to some serious issues.

Here's the kicker: boundaries aren't just for the kids. You've got to set them for yourself, too. I remember one evening, my toddler was playing a game on my phone, and I thought, "I'll just check my email." Three hours later, I was knee-deep in a rabbit hole of TikTok videos. Oops! Talk about losing track of time.

So, how do you create those boundaries? Here's a handy list:

1. **Set Screen Time Limits**: Decide how much screen time is appropriate for your child based on their age and developmental needs. The American Academy of Pediatrics suggests no more than one hour of high-quality programming for kids aged 2 to 5. For older kids, it's all about balance.

2. **Create Device-Free Zones**: Designate certain areas in your home, like the dining room or bedrooms, as screen-free zones. This encourages family time and helps kids develop other interests.

3. **Establish Tech Curfews**: Set a time when all devices go to bed—yep, even yours! This can help improve sleep quality for everyone in the house. Trust me, your future self will thank you when you're not up at 2 AM binge-watching that new series.

4. **Model Healthy Usage**: Kids are like little sponges, soaking up everything you do. If you want them to limit their screen time, you've got to lead by example. Put your phone down during family meals and engage in conversation.

Now that we've got some boundaries in place, let's talk about understanding the impact of technology on development. This is crucial because, believe it or not, what they're watching and playing can shape their brains in ways we're just starting to understand.

Studies show that excessive screen time can lead to issues like attention problems, sleep disturbances, and even anxiety. Yikes! It's like handing your kid a loaded water gun and hoping they don't spray the neighbor's cat.

But it's not all doom and gloom. Technology can also be a powerful tool for learning and creativity. The key is to choose quality content. Think of it like selecting the right ingredients for a recipe. You wouldn't throw just anything into a pot and hope for the best, right?

Here are some tips for selecting high-quality content:

- **Look for Educational Programs**: Shows like "Sesame Street" or "Bluey" not only entertain but also teach valuable lessons about social skills and problem-solving.

- **Encourage Interactive Play**: Apps and games that require critical thinking and creativity can be beneficial. Look for ones that promote active engagement rather than passive consumption.

- **Balance Screen Time with Real-World Experiences**: Encourage your child to explore the outdoors, read books, and engage in hands-on activities. This helps develop their imagination and social skills.

Now, let's shift gears and talk about encouraging balanced media consumption. Think of media consumption like a well-balanced diet. You wouldn't feed your kid nothing but candy, right? They need fruits, veggies, and all that good stuff. The same goes for their media intake.

Here's how to encourage balance:

1. **Create a Media Plan**: Work with your child to create a weekly media plan that includes educational content, recreational screen time, and offline activities. This gives them

ownership and helps them understand the importance of balance.

2. **Engage in Co-Viewing**: Whenever possible, watch shows or play games together. This opens up opportunities for discussion and helps you gauge whether the content is appropriate.

3. **Encourage Critical Thinking**: After watching a show or playing a game, ask your child what they thought about it. Questions like "What did you learn?" or "How would you feel if that happened to you?" can spark meaningful conversations.

4. **Incorporate Tech Breaks**: Just like we need breaks from work, kids need breaks from screens. Encourage them to take short breaks every hour to stretch, grab a snack, or just chill out.

Remember, the goal here isn't to eliminate technology altogether but to create a healthy relationship with it. It's all about finding that sweet spot where screens enhance their lives rather than control them.

So, what's the takeaway from all this? Setting boundaries, understanding the impact of technology, and encouraging balanced consumption are key to navigating this digital landscape. It's a learning curve, no doubt about it. But with a little patience and a sprinkle of humor, you can help your child thrive in this tech-savvy world.

And hey, don't forget to give yourself some grace along the way. Parenting is a wild ride, and we're all just trying to figure it out as we go. So, take a deep breath, put on your favorite playlist, and remember: you've got this!

Chapter 10

Cultivating Emotional Intelligence in Your Child

Let's get into the real deal about emotional intelligence, or EQ if you wanna sound hip. What's it all about? Simply put, it's understanding and managing feelings—yours and your kid's. Why bother? Well, studies show that kids with high EQs usually ace school, have better friendships, and are just happier overall. So, let's get to work on boosting that emotional smarts!

First up, we gotta teach our kids the lingo of feelings. Think about it: you wouldn't toss your kid into a foreign country without some kind of guide, right? So why let them wander through their feelings without the right words? Here's a cool trick: make an "emotion wheel." You can snag a template online or just doodle one yourself. Fill it with words like "happy," "frustrated," "excited," and "anxious." Sit down with your kid and go through it. Ask them how they feel in different situations. For instance, "How do you feel when you lose a game?" or "What's it like when you get a new toy?"

Encourage them to spill those feelings. You might say, "It's totally fine to feel sad. Let's chat about it!" This kind of open talk not only boosts their emotional vocabulary but also tells them their feelings matter. Seriously, it's like handing them a superpower. They'll learn to pinpoint and express their emotions instead of throwing a fit or sulking in silence.

Now, let's chat about role-playing. This isn't just for drama geeks; it's a killer way to build empathy. You know those moments when your kid doesn't quite get why their friend is upset? Enter role-playing. Set up some scenarios they might face—like a buddy feeling left out or a sibling getting teased. Act it out together. You take on the role of the friend, and let them practice how to respond.

"Okay, I'm your friend who just lost my favorite toy. What do you say?" This isn't just about acting; it's about feeling. It helps them step into someone else's shoes. And the best part? It's not just about saying the right thing; it's about grasping the emotions behind those words. You're not just teaching them empathy; you're giving them tools for real-life social situations.

Now, let's shift gears to perspective-taking. This one's huge. Getting your child to see things from someone else's angle can be a game changer. It's like teaching them to read between the lines of social interactions. Ask questions that get them thinking. "How do you think your friend felt when you didn't invite them to play?" or "What do you think your teacher feels when the class is noisy?"

By nudging this kind of thinking, you're helping them build social skills that'll stick with them for life. Kids who can take perspective are usually more compassionate and understanding. Plus, it helps prevent conflicts. If they can grasp how someone else feels, they're less likely to lash out or hurt others.

Wondering how to make this fun? Turn it into a game! Use board games or video games that need teamwork and communication. After a game, ask about what went down. "How'd it feel when you lost that round?" or "What could we do differently next time?" This kind of reflection keeps the convo rolling and reinforces the lessons learned.

And hey, don't sleep on the power of storytelling. Kids are suckers for stories, and they're a fab way to illustrate emotional concepts. Read books together that dive into feelings and social situations. After reading, chat about the characters' emotions. "Why do you think the character acted that way?" or "How would you feel in that situation?" This can spark some deep convos and help your kid relate to others' emotions.

As you're working on this stuff, remember to lead by example. Kids are like little sponges; they soak up everything we do. If you want them to express their feelings, you gotta show them how. Share your feelings openly. "I'm feeling a bit stressed today, but talking about it helps." This teaches them it's okay to let it all out.

And let's keep it real. Parenting's a tough gig, and we're all just winging it. You won't nail it every time, and that's totally cool. The key is you're making an effort. Celebrate those little wins. Did your kid express their feelings instead of throwing a tantrum? High five! Did they show empathy to a friend? Give 'em a pat on the back!

Alright, let's wrap this up with some quick action steps you can take right now.

1. Make an emotion wheel together.

2. Set aside time for role-playing different scenarios.

3. Encourage perspective-taking through questions and games.

4. Read stories about emotions and chat about them.

5. Show emotional expression in your own life.

By tackling these steps, you're not just teaching your kid about feelings; you're equipping them with the skills to thrive in a world that can be pretty overwhelming.

In the end, nurturing emotional intelligence in your child is like planting a garden. It takes time, patience, and a little TLC. But with the right tools and strategies, you'll be blown away by how your kid blossoms into an emotionally aware and empathetic person. So, roll up your sleeves, dig in, and let's grow some emotional smarts together!

Chapter 11

Fostering a Growth Mindset

Alright, let's dive into the nitty-gritty of fostering a growth mindset in your kiddos. This is the stuff that'll set them up for success, not just in school but in life. Think of it as equipping them with a Swiss Army knife of skills to tackle whatever comes their way. So, grab a cup of coffee (or whatever gets you through the day), and let's get started!

First up, let's chat about the power of praise and constructive feedback. Now, I know what you might be thinking: "Isn't all praise good praise?" Well, not quite. Let me tell you a little story. Back when I was a kid, my mom would say, "You're so smart!" every time I aced a test. I felt like a genius, but here's the kicker—I started to think that if I wasn't perfect, I wasn't smart. Talk about pressure!

Instead, what if we praised the effort? "Wow, you worked really hard on that project!" or "I love how you kept trying even when it got tough!" This kind of praise teaches kids that it's not just about being smart; it's about putting in the work. When they hear, "You can improve with practice," they start to believe it. They'll be more likely to take on challenges, knowing that their effort matters more than the end result.

Constructive feedback is just as crucial. Let's say your kiddo brings home a drawing that looks like a tornado hit a crayon factory. Instead of saying, "That's great!" and leaving it at that, try something like, "I really love the colors you used! What if we added some more shapes to make it pop?" This way, they feel encouraged to explore their creativity while learning how to improve. It's all about building a safe space for them to grow and learn.

Now, let's move on to encouraging a love for learning and exploration. Imagine this: you're at a museum, and your kid is glued to the dinosaur exhibit, eyes wide with wonder. You could easily breeze past and say, "Let's go see the mummies," but hold on! This is a GOLDEN opportunity. Ask them questions like, "What do you think they ate?" or "How do you think they lived?"

When kids see you engaging with their interests, it sparks their curiosity. They'll learn that exploration isn't just for school—it's a lifelong adventure. Encourage them to ask questions, dig deeper, and seek answers. Set up scavenger hunts, or let them choose a new hobby. Maybe they want to learn how to cook, or perhaps they're itching to try their hand at gardening. Whatever it is, support their journey!

And here's a little tip: lead by example. Share your own love for learning. If you're reading a book, let them see you absorbed in it. Talk about what you're learning and how it excites you. Show them that learning doesn't stop when you leave the classroom; it's a daily practice.

Now, let's tackle the big one: overcoming the fear of failure through resilience. This is where the magic happens, folks! We've all been there—facing a challenge that makes us want to crawl under a rock. But here's the deal: failure is NOT the end of the world. In fact, it's a stepping stone to success.

When I was in high school, I bombed my first math test. I mean, it was bad. I felt like I'd just been hit by a freight train. But my dad said something that stuck with me: "Failure is just feedback." At first, I thought he was nuts. But then it clicked. I realized that failing at something just meant I had room to grow.

Teach your kids that it's okay to fail. In fact, it's necessary! Encourage them to try new things, even if they're not sure they'll succeed. Celebrate the effort, not just the outcome. If they strike out in baseball, say, "Hey, you swung for the fences! Let's practice together."

And here's a little exercise for you: create a "failure wall" at home. Whenever someone in the family experiences a setback, write it down and discuss it. What did you learn? How can you improve next time? This not only normalizes failure but also builds resilience.

Now, let's wrap this up with some actionable steps. Here's a quick checklist to get you started on fostering that growth mindset:

1. **Praise Effort Over Results**: Make a conscious effort to focus on hard work and determination rather than just achievements.

2. **Provide Constructive Feedback**: Offer specific suggestions for improvement instead of vague compliments.

3. **Encourage Exploration**: Ask questions that spark curiosity and let your child take the lead in their learning journey.

4. **Model Lifelong Learning**: Share your own learning experiences and interests with your child.

5. **Normalize Failure**: Discuss setbacks openly and create a safe space for your child to express their feelings about failure.

6. **Create a Failure Wall**: Document failures and lessons learned to foster resilience and growth.

7. **Celebrate Small Wins**: No matter how small, recognize and celebrate progress.

8. **Set Challenges Together**: Take on new activities as a family. Whether it's learning a new sport or trying a new recipe, tackle challenges together!

Remember, you're not just raising kids; you're raising future adults who will face a world full of challenges. Equip them with the tools they need to thrive. It's a wild ride, but with a growth mindset, they'll be ready to take it on—one dinosaur exhibit at a time!

Chapter 12

Parenting Through Transitions

Life's a rollercoaster, right? One moment, you're cruising, and then—wham!—you hit a bump that sends you spinning into a whole new reality. Whether it's a divorce, moving to a new city, or changing jobs, transitions can feel like juggling flaming torches while riding a unicycle. And guess what? Your kids are right there, trying to keep their balance too. So, how do we get through these choppy waters without capsizing? Let's dive in!

First, let's chat about prepping for those big life changes. Imagine this: you've decided to move your family from sunny California to the snowy Midwest. That's a hefty shift, right? Boxes everywhere, and your kids are probably feeling both excited and scared. Here's the scoop: KIDS ARE RESILIENT, but they need your help to process what's going down.

Communicate Openly: Have a sit-down with your kids about the move. Don't sugarcoat it, but don't go overboard either. Keep it age-appropriate. For the little ones, say something like, "We're moving to a new place where we'll have new adventures!" For the older kids, share your feelings too. It's cool to admit you're nervous. This builds trust and shows them it's okay to feel a mix of emotions.

Involve Them in the Process: Give your kids a sense of control. Let them help pack their stuff, choose their new rooms, or even look up fun activities in the new town. It's like giving them a front-row seat at the family meeting. Trust me, it makes a huge difference.

Create a Transition Plan: Kids thrive on routine, so try to keep some things consistent. Maybe it's the same bedtime story or a family game night. When you're uprooting their world, maintaining some stability can help them feel grounded.

Now, let's switch gears and tackle something heavier: supporting your child through grief and loss. This is tough, but it's part of life. Whether it's losing a pet, a family member, or a familiar environment, kids need guidance to navigate those feelings.

Acknowledge Their Feelings: Kids might not always find the words for their grief, but that doesn't mean they're not feeling it.

Encourage them to share their thoughts and listen without judgment. You might say, "It's okay to feel sad. I feel sad too. Let's talk about it." Validating their emotions helps them process what they're going through.

Share Your Own Grief: This can be hard, but showing your vulnerability can be powerful. Share your feelings and memories. You could say, "I miss Grandma too. Remember when she used to bake cookies with us? Let's talk about our favorite memories." This opens the door for conversation and shows them that grief is a shared experience.

Create a Memory Ritual: This could be anything from planting a tree in memory of a loved one to making a scrapbook of memories. It gives your child a tangible way to express their feelings and keeps the memory alive in a positive light.

Finally, let's talk about keeping stability during transitions. Think of it as building a sturdy bridge over choppy waters. Here's how you can do it:

Establish Routines: Routines are like GPS for kids. They give direction and security. Stick to familiar routines as much as you can, especially during big changes. Breakfast, homework time, and bedtime rituals should stay consistent. It's like the comfort food of parenting!

Encourage Social Connections: Help your child maintain friendships, whether through video calls, playdates, or social media. If you're moving, encourage them to reach out to old friends and make new ones. A strong support network can make all the difference.

Be Patient: Remember, it's okay for your child to take time to adjust. Don't rush the process. If they're having a rough day, acknowledge it and offer extra hugs. Sometimes, a little TLC goes a long way.

Transitions are like those annoying pop-up ads on the internet. You can't dodge 'em, but you can learn to deal with them effectively. Embrace the chaos, communicate openly, and remember you're not alone in this. Parenting is a journey, and every bump in the road is a chance to grow—for you and your kids.

So, as you navigate these transitions, keep these strategies handy. You've got this! Your child looks to you for guidance, and by showing them how to handle life's changes, you're teaching them resilience and adaptability. And let's be real—those are skills they'll need for life.

Now, before we wrap this up, let's reflect. Think about a transition you've faced. How'd you handle it? What'd you learn? Use those experiences to inform your parenting. After all, you're not just raising kids; you're raising future adults. Equip them with the tools they need to tackle life's transitions head-on.

In closing, remember that every transition is a chance for growth. Embrace the journey, and don't stress over every little bump. Life's too short for that. So, buckle up, hold on tight, and let's navigate these twists and turns together!

Chapter 13

The Importance of Family Rituals

When I think about family rituals, I can't help but chuckle at the image of my Aunt Karen trying to get everyone to participate in her "family dance-off" at Thanksgiving. Picture it: a group of relatives, half of them still in their food coma from the turkey, and Aunt Karen, bless her heart, busting out the moves like she's auditioning for a reality show. It was chaotic, hilarious, and a little embarrassing, but you know what? It was OUR chaos. And that's what family rituals are all about—creating those unique, meaningful traditions that stick with us long after the last slice of pie is gone.

Creating meaningful family traditions is like planting seeds in a garden. You water them with love, laughter, and a sprinkle of awkwardness, and before you know it, they blossom into cherished memories. Whether it's Taco Tuesdays, movie marathons, or Saturday morning pancake flips, these rituals become the glue that holds us together. They provide a sense of stability in our ever-changing lives. When the world feels like it's spinning out of control, those little traditions are our anchor.

Now, let's talk about the impact of rituals on family bonding. It's simple: shared experiences create connections. When you gather around the table for a weekly family game night, you're not just playing Monopoly (which, let's be honest, can get a little cutthroat). You're building trust, fostering communication, and creating a safe space where everyone feels valued. Think of it like a team-building exercise, but with more snacks and fewer trust falls.

Rituals also help us navigate the tough stuff. Life isn't all rainbows and butterflies. Sometimes it's more like thunderstorms and soggy socks. But having rituals in place gives us a framework to lean on during those storms. For instance, after a rough day at school, we'd gather for our "feelings circle" where everyone shared their highs and lows. It was a safe zone—no judgment, just love. And let me tell you, those moments of vulnerability? They strengthened our bonds in ways I can't even begin to describe.

Now, you might be wondering, how do you actually go about creating these family rituals? Well, here's a little roadmap to get you started:

1. **Identify What Matters**: What do you and your family enjoy doing together? Is it cooking, hiking, or binge-watching the latest

Netflix series? Pinpoint those activities that bring you joy.

2. **Make It Regular**: Consistency is key. Set aside a specific day or time each week for your ritual. It doesn't have to be fancy; even a weekly walk around the block can become a cherished tradition.

3. **Involve Everyone**: Get the kids involved in the planning. Ask for their input on what rituals they'd like to create. This not only empowers them but also makes them feel like they're part of the process.

4. **Be Flexible**: Life happens. Sometimes, the kids might have soccer practice, or you might be too exhausted after a long week. That's okay! Adapt and adjust your rituals as needed. The goal is to create connection, not stress.

5. **Capture the Moments**: Take photos, write down funny stories, or create a family scrapbook. These tangible memories will serve as a reminder of the fun times you've shared.

Now, let's dive into how rituals can instill values and memories. Think of rituals as the delivery system for life lessons. When you engage in activities that reflect your family's values—like volunteering together or sharing gratitude at dinner—you're not just having fun; you're teaching your kids what matters. It's like sneaking vegetables into a delicious smoothie. They're getting the nutrients without even realizing it!

For example, every December, my family has a "giving week." We pick a charity, gather supplies, and spend a day volunteering. Not only does it feel good to give back, but it also teaches the kids the importance of empathy and community. Plus, they get to see firsthand how their actions can make a difference. That's a lesson that sticks with them far longer than any lecture ever could.

And let's not forget about the memories! Rituals are the fabric of our family history. They're the stories we'll tell at future family gatherings. Remember that time we tried to bake cookies and ended up with a kitchen disaster? Those moments of laughter and mishaps become the highlights of our family narrative. They remind us that it's not about perfection; it's about connection.

Now, I get it. You might be thinking, "But my family is too busy for rituals!" Here's the thing: you don't have to carve out a whole day for family bonding. Start small. Even a 15-minute bedtime routine can be impactful. Read a book, share one thing you're grateful for, or just chat about your day. It's about quality, not quantity.

As you embark on this journey of creating family rituals, keep in mind that it's not a one-size-fits-all approach. What works for one family might not work for another. So, feel free to experiment! If Taco Tuesdays turn into Taco Thursdays, roll with it. The goal is to foster connection, not stress about sticking to a schedule.

So, let's recap:

- Family rituals create meaningful traditions that provide stability.

- Shared experiences strengthen family bonds and foster communication.

- Rituals instill values and create lasting memories.

- Start small, involve everyone, and be flexible.

In closing, I want to encourage you to embrace the beauty of family rituals. They're the heartbeat of your family life, the stories that will echo through generations. So go ahead, grab your loved ones, and start creating those moments that will become the fabric of your family's story. You've got this!

And who knows? Maybe one day, your kids will be laughing about that time you tried to recreate Aunt Karen's dance-off at Thanksgiving. And that, my friend, is what it's all about.

Chapter 14

Teaming Up with Teachers

Getting chummy with your kid's teachers isn't just a bonus; it's crucial for your child's success. Think of it as forming a dynamic duo. You and the educators are in the ring, battling for your kid's future. You might be wondering, "How do I kick off this partnership?" Well, hang tight, 'cause I'm about to drop some wisdom that'll help you forge a solid connection with the folks who spend all day with your little one.

First things first, get to know the teachers and staff. This isn't just about small talk during drop-off. Show up at school events, volunteer for activities, or even shoot them an email to say hi. When you put a face to a name, it's like opening a door to better communication. Seriously, teachers dig it when parents show interest. It makes them feel appreciated and opens up lines for discussing your child's needs.

Now, let's dive into understanding your child's learning style. Every kid learns differently. Some are visual learners, others soak it up through listening, and some need to get hands-on. Ever tried teaching a cat to fetch? Yeah, good luck with that. Same goes for teaching your kid in a way that doesn't click with how they learn. So, how do you figure this out?

Start by watching your child. What gets them excited? Do they light up when they're doodling or building something? Do they prefer listening to stories or reading them? Once you've got a grip on their style, share it with their teachers. This way, you can work together to create an environment where your kid can thrive. It's like cooking; you need the right ingredients to whip up something tasty.

Next up, let's chat about advocating for your child's needs at school. This is where you become the superhero in their story. You might think, "But I don't wanna be that parent." Well, sometimes, you gotta be that parent. It's not about stirring the pot; it's about making sure your kid gets what they need to succeed.

Start by getting clued in. Know the school's policies, understand the resources available, and don't hesitate to ask questions. If your kid's struggling, reach out to their teacher and voice your concerns. Be specific. Instead of saying, "My child is having a hard time," try, "I've noticed my child struggles with reading comprehension. Can we brainstorm some strategies?" This shows you're engaged and proactive, which teachers appreciate.

Sometimes, you might need to push a bit harder. If you feel your kid isn't getting the support they need, don't shy away from asking for an Individualized Education Plan (IEP) or a 504 Plan. These plans can offer accommodations that help your child thrive. Remember, you're not just advocating for them; you're advocating for their future.

Here's a quick rundown on how to team up with educators effectively:

1. Build Relationships

    - Attend school events and volunteer.

    - Keep communication open and regular.

2. Understand Learning Styles

- Observe what your child enjoys and excels at.

- Share your insights with teachers.

3. Advocate for Needs

- Be informed about school policies and resources.

- Bring up concerns with specific examples.

- Don't hesitate to ask for extra support when needed.

And let's not forget about teamwork. You and the educators are on the same side. When you approach conversations with a collaborative vibe, solutions come easier. It's like being in a band: everyone's got their role, and when you harmonize, the music is sweet.

Now, let's throw in a bit of humor. Picture this: you're at a parent-teacher conference, feeling all jittery. Your palms are sweaty, and you're replaying all the times your kid forgot their homework. Instead of letting nerves take over, remind yourself that teachers are just people too. They've got their own kids, their own issues, and they're probably just as anxious about meeting you as you are about meeting them. So, take a deep breath, smile, and remember you're all in this together.

In the end, teaming up with educators is about building relationships, understanding your child's unique learning style, and advocating for their needs. It's not brain surgery, but it does take some effort. So, roll up your sleeves, dive in, and remember you're your child's best advocate. Together with their teachers, you can create a space where your kid can truly shine. And hey, if you ever feel swamped, just think of it like a potluck dinner: everyone brings something to the table, and together, you create a feast of knowledge and support for your child. Now, go out there and be the parent your kid needs!

Chapter 15

Celebrating Uniqueness and Diversity

Alright, let's dive into something super important and beautiful in our parenting journey: celebrating our kids' uniqueness and the colorful diversity around us. I don't know about you, but when I was a kid, all I wanted was to fit in. Who doesn't wanna be part of the "in" crowd, right? But here's a thought—what if we flipped that? What if we taught our kids to embrace their true selves and appreciate what makes others different? Buckle up, 'cause we're gonna explore how to do just that!

First off, let's honor our kids' individuality. Each kid is like a snowflake—totally unique! You might have one little Picasso, scribbling on everything in sight, while another's a mini Einstein, asking why the sky's blue. Instead of trying to mold them into some cookie-cutter version of a "perfect" kid, let's celebrate what makes them tick.

Imagine this: take a moment to ask your child what they're into. You might find out they're passionate about something totally unexpected. Maybe they love coding video games or collecting rocks. Whatever it is, encourage them! Give them the tools they need—books, art supplies, or a science kit subscription. This sends a clear message: "Hey, you do you! I'm here to back you up."

Now, let's chat about teaching respect and appreciation for differences. It's kinda like teaching a kid to ride a bike. You don't just toss them on and hope they don't crash, right? You guide them, hold the handlebars until they find their balance. Same goes for understanding diversity.

Start small. Use everyday moments to spark conversations about differences. Maybe you're watching a movie, and a character comes from a different background. Ask your kid what they think about that character's story. Why do they act that way? What can we learn from them? It's all about planting seeds of curiosity and respect.

Lead by example, too. When you meet someone different—whether in looks, culture, or beliefs—show your child how to engage respectfully. Share your own experiences and how diversity adds richness to our lives. I remember the first time I met someone from another country. I was nervous, but it blossomed into a beautiful friendship. Sharing stories like that helps your kid see the value in diversity.

Encouraging open discussions about diversity is key. You might be wondering, "How do I even start that convo?" It's easier than you think. Create a safe space for dialogue. Let your kid know it's cool to ask questions and share their thoughts. You could say, "I love hearing your opinions! What do you think about this?"

And hey, don't dodge tough topics. If something pops up in the news or at school that's tricky, tackle it head-on. You can say, "I noticed you seemed upset about what happened. Want to talk about it?" This shows your kid that discussing complex issues is normal and their feelings matter.

To make these chats more engaging, use books or movies that celebrate diversity. There are tons of great resources! For instance, "Last Stop on Market Street" by Matt de la Peña is a fantastic story that highlights different perspectives. After reading, ask your kid how they relate to the characters. What did they learn? This encourages empathy and reinforces that everyone's story is worth telling.

Another fun idea? Host a diversity night at home! Pick a country, whip up a traditional dish, and learn a few phrases in that language. You could even watch a movie from that culture. It's a fun way to dive into the richness of diversity while bonding as a family. Plus, who doesn't love taco night?

As we celebrate our kids' uniqueness and the diversity around us, let's not ignore the challenges that come with it. Sometimes, kids face bullying or exclusion because they're different. Be proactive! Teach your child how to stand up for themselves and others. Role-play scenarios where they might need to defend a friend or express their feelings. Equip them with the words they need to advocate for themselves and others.

And don't forget to share your own vulnerabilities. I once faced bullying in school for being different. I told my kids about it, and it sparked a discussion about resilience and empathy. They learned that everyone has their battles, and that's what makes us human.

Let's wrap this up with some actionable steps. Here's a quick list to keep you on track:

1. Embrace Individuality: Celebrate your child's unique interests. Encourage them to explore their passions.

2. Teach Respect: Use everyday moments to discuss differences. Lead by example and show respect for all people.

3. Encourage Dialogue: Create a safe space for discussions about diversity. Let your child know it's okay to ask questions.

4. Use Resources: Incorporate books and movies that celebrate diversity into your family time. Discuss what you learn together.

5. Host Diversity Nights: Make learning about different cultures fun! Cook meals, watch films, and immerse yourselves in new experiences.

6. Teach Advocacy: Role-play scenarios where your child might need to stand up for

themselves or others. Equip them with the language they need.

7. Share Vulnerabilities: Open up about your own experiences with diversity. This builds empathy and connection.

Now, I know this might seem like a lot, but take it one step at a time. Celebrate those little victories along the way! And remember, you're not just raising kids; you're raising compassionate, open-minded humans who will contribute to a better world. That's the ultimate goal, right?

So, let's get out there and celebrate the beautiful uniqueness of our children and the rich diversity of our world. It's a journey worth taking, and I promise, you'll be amazed at the growth—both in your kids and in yourself. Let's make this parenting gig not just about survival, but about thriving together!

Index

* 9 7 9 8 3 3 0 6 6 0 0 6 3 *